LEATHERWORKER

MAKERS AND ARTISANS

JOSH GREGORY

Published in the United States of America by Cherry Lake Publishing Group
Ann Arbor, Michigan
www.cherrylakepublishing.com

Reading Adviser: Beth Walker Gambro, MS, Ed., Reading Consultant, Yorkville, IL

Photo Credits: © Deviatov Aleksei/Shutterstock.com, cover, 1, 24; © Dean Drobot/Shutterstock.com, 5;
© Lithiumphoto/Shutterstock.com, 6; © Commercial RAF/Shutterstock.com, 8; © Olaf Speier/
Shutterstock.com, 9; © SeventyFour/Shutterstock.com, 10, 14, 23; © Monkey Business Images/
Shutterstock.com, 13; © Deviatov Aleksei/Shutterstock.com, 17; © AlexanderLipko/Shutterstock.
com, 18; © Iakov Filimonov/Shutterstock.com, 21; © MintImages/Shutterstock.com, 27;
© UfaBizPhoto/Shutterstock.com, 28

Library of Congress Cataloging-in-Publication Data

Names: Gregory, Josh, author.
Title: Leatherworker / by Josh Gregory.
Description: Ann Arbor, Michigan : Cherry Lake Publishing, [2022] | Series: Makers and artisans |
    Includes bibliographical references and index. | Audience: Grades 4-6
Identifiers: LCCN 2021007870 (print) | LCCN 2021007871 (ebook) | ISBN 9781534187269 (hardcover) |
    ISBN 9781534188662 (paperback) | ISBN 9781534190061 (pdf) | ISBN 9781534191464 (ebook)
Subjects: LCSH: Leatherwork—Vocational guidance—Juvenile literature. | Leather industry and trade—
    Vocational guidance—Juvenile literature.
Classification: LCC TT290 .G83 2022 (print) | LCC TT290 (ebook) | DDC 338.4/7675023—dc23
LC record available at https://lccn.loc.gov/2021007870
LC ebook record available at https://lccn.loc.gov/2021007871

Cherry Lake Publishing Group would like to acknowledge the work of the Partnership for 21st Century
Learning, a Network of Battelle for Kids. Please visit http://www.battelleforkids.org/networks/p21
for more information.

Printed in the United States of America
Corporate Graphics

ABOUT THE AUTHOR

Josh Gregory is the author of more than 150 books for kids. He has written about everything
from animals to technology to history. A graduate of the University of Missouri-Columbia,
he currently lives in Chicago, Illinois.

TABLE OF CONTENTS

CHAPTER 1
Skin Deep 4

CHAPTER 2
The Leatherworking Lifestyle 12

CHAPTER 3
A Crafty Career 20

CHAPTER 4
Looking at Leather 26

CRAFT ACTIVITY 30

FIND OUT MORE 31

GLOSSARY 32

INDEX 32

Skin Deep

Spread across the **artisan**'s workspace, the piece of leather looks something like a smooth, hairless rug. It's wide and flat. But as the leatherworker starts cutting and sewing, the leather takes on a whole new shape. It's a slow process, but you soon see the beginnings of a beautiful handmade wallet.

Leatherworking is an ancient art form with a history dating back at least 7,000 years. People have relied on leather to make everything from clothing and furniture to books and footballs. This **versatile** material is popular for many reasons. When properly crafted, it's very durable and long-lasting. Used in clothing, it can keep wearers warm and dry while offering protection from injuries. It also has a unique appearance that can improve over time with good care.

[21ST CENTURY SKILLS LIBRARY]

When properly crafted, leather is durable and long-lasting.

Leather is a popular material for shoes.

Leather is an animal product. Long ago, ancient people realized that animal skins' natural protective properties made it useful for all kinds of things. When people hunted, they used as many of an animal's body parts as possible. Meat was food, but bones could be turned into tools, and organs could be turned into bags for carrying things. Skins worked best as clothing or shelter.

Much like meat or other animal products, skins start to rot if left in their natural state. They will smell bad and eventually fall apart. This means they must be preserved before they can be used to make long-lasting items. The process of preserving an animal skin and turning it into useful leather is called tanning.

Leather comes in many different colors.

Traditionally, this process usually (but not always) began by removing any hair or fur from the **hide**. The skins were then hung to dry in the sun. To soften the dried skins, leather makers rubbed them with animal fat and pounded them with blunt tools. Afterward, the skins could be preserved by treating them with salt or wood smoke. These substances kill off **bacteria** and other substances that can cause **organic** materials to rot. It's not a coincidence that the same processes have long been used to preserve meat!

Leatherworkers must be comfortable with sewing machines.

Leatherworking requires many different tools.

The process of making leather has changed a lot throughout history. Many new ways to tan hides have been discovered, resulting in a wider variety of available leathers. And beginning in the 1800s, many traditional manufacturing practices were modernized to take advantage of new machines. This made the process of cutting and sewing leather easier and less expensive. Many companies began to mass-produce inexpensive leather goods. Today, it's easy to find cheaply made leather bags, shoes, or jackets at stores. But these items rarely display the high quality for which leather was once famous. To make inexpensive leather items affordable, they might be made from thin, easily damaged leather, or sewn together poorly by a machine.

Despite these changes in the leather industry, many artisans aim to create high-quality items by hand from the finest leathers. Their customers are often willing to pay handsomely for goods that will stand the test of time.

A Controversial Material

While leather was once an important tool for survival, it's mostly seen as a luxury item today. Because leather production requires animals to be killed, many people think it is wrong to continue using this material in modern times. Most things that were once almost always made of leather, such as shoes or sports equipment, can now easily be made using materials that don't come from animals.

Some leather fans argue that alternative materials just aren't the same. Nothing looks or feels quite like a high-quality leather item. If you love the look of real leather but you don't want to support animal products, one option is to seek out used items. Because leather is so durable, clothes and furniture can last for many decades. In some cases, vintage items can even look better than brand-new ones. Another possibility is to find leatherworkers who make things from recycled leather pieces.

CHAPTER 2

The Leatherworking Lifestyle

Each decision a leatherworker makes when creating something has a visible effect on the final product. This means there is a lot of pressure to do things right. But as a result of this hard work, each and every object is unique. If you want to put your personal touch on objects that people use every day, this could be just the right craft for you.

The first step of any leatherworking project is simply deciding what to make. This could mean following the same set of steps you've followed many times before or experimenting with

Working with leather is all about careful attention to detail.

something new. Different steps are required to make different things. For example, making a belt is much simpler than creating handmade shoes from scratch. For custom projects, a leatherworker might need to take a customer's wants into account. Other times, the leatherworker has free range to express their creativity.

The next step is to design a pattern and plan the project. This could start with a simple sketch in a notebook. From there, the leatherworker plans the size and shape of the different pieces of

Leatherworkers must work carefully when cutting pieces in order to not waste any leather.

leather needed to assemble the final product. They might draw and cut sample pieces from paper or cloth to make sure everything works correctly before cutting up real leather. If all goes according to plan, these samples can later be used to trace when preparing the leather.

The world is filled with many unique kinds of leather, and tanners continue to come up with new varieties. Some hides are better suited to certain projects than others. For example, a thick piece of horsehide is heavy and stiff. It might be great for making a tough motorcycle jacket that needs to stand up to a lot of wear. But if a leatherworker wanted to make a pair of stylish, comfortable gloves, they might choose a piece of soft lambskin instead.

Sometimes, the choice of leather just comes down to how it looks and feels. Some leathers have a pebbled texture that feels bumpy. Others are completely smooth. Suede is a type of leather with a soft, velvety texture. Some leathers crease easily when bent, while others move like cloth.

Once the artisan chooses a piece of leather, it's time to plan out how pieces will be cut out. Animal hides aren't uniform in shape. Each one is slightly different, and they don't have straight edges like fabric. The leatherworker must look closely at the hide to figure the most **efficient** way to cut pieces needed for each pattern. It would be simple to just start outlining and cutting wherever there was enough room. But this would result in a lot of wasted leather.

The goal is to get as much use out of each hide as possible. In many cases, it's important to make sure all the pieces of each object come from the same hide. Otherwise, there might be slight variation in color or texture between different parts of the object. The process of cutting leather pieces from a hide is sometimes called clicking. This is because of the sound leather-cutting hand tools make.

Taking Care

Leather requires regular care to stay in good condition. At the very least, this means keeping it clean. Built-up dirt, salt, and other grime can damage the leather. If you wear leather shoes, it is a great idea to wipe them with a damp cloth every time you take them off.

Leather can also dry out and start to crack after a while. Regularly applying leather conditioner can solve this problem. Leather conditioner works a lot like lotion. It moisturizes and keeps the leather in good shape.

Even well-cared-for leather can start to lose its color and shine over time. Depending on the object and its owner's personal tastes, this might be a good thing. A well-worn leather jacket or boots can look better after they are broken in, much like a favorite pair of jeans. But sometimes, you might want leather to stay shiny and look new. In many cases, you can preserve this look by polishing the leather. For example, people who wear handmade leather dress shoes tend to polish them regularly.

Like any craft, leatherworking requires knowledge and practice.

The best way to start is to work on some basic leatherworking projects at home. You can buy inexpensive pieces of leather and basic tools at craft stores or order them online. All kinds of instructions and tutorials for making basic items such as belts, wallets, and phone cases are available online. Better yet, you might have a friend or relative who has some experience with leatherworking. Ask them to show you how it is done.

The next step might be to take some leatherworking classes. Some are held online, while others might be offered through crafting centers or leatherworking shops in your area. Most are focused on creating a certain type of item, such as wallets or bags.

An **apprenticeship** is a common way to make the move from hobbyist to professional leatherworker. An apprentice works under the guidance of an experienced leatherworker. At first, they might do basic tasks to help out around the shop, such as cleaning up or organizing supplies. But as they learn more, they get more responsibility. While an apprenticeship is an excellent way to learn and make connections with other leatherworkers, it isn't

Leatherworkers etch designs into the leather using sharp tools.

a requirement to start working as a leatherworker. In fact, there are no real requirements at all if you have enough skill and talent.

Some types of leatherworking require specialized skills. For example, **upholstering** furniture is very different from making belts. Those who want to make leather clothing need all the knowledge and training of a clothing designer, plus leatherworking skills. If you want to create shoes, you'll need to train as a **cobbler**.

During the tanning process, leathers can be changed from
a natural skin tone to just about any color imaginable.

Many jobs provide opportunities for leatherworkers to practice their trade. Established companies that manufacture clothing might hire leatherworkers to design or assemble leather goods. Or a local repair shop might hire assistants to help. Of course, leatherworkers always have the option to start their own businesses. They might also make deals with store owners to stock their goods in physical shops.

Balancing the Books

Leatherworkers who decide to go into business selling their own creations need to be very careful when managing money. They need to keep track of how much their materials cost and how much time they spend working. This is how to determine a fair price for their creations. If they set the price too low or fail to sell enough items, they could lose money. Knowledge of basic business principles can really come in handy. If you're interested in starting your own business, it pays to do some research beforehand and make sure you are prepared to take on the responsibility. A successful leatherworker can make a lot of money, but it's not guaranteed.

Looking at Leather

Most leather goods are common, everyday objects. You've probably seen countless brown leather belts or wallets. But some leather creations are made to stand out.

Some leather artisans like to work with **exotic** leathers. Just about any animal skin can be turned into leather, from snakes and crocodiles to ostriches and kangaroos. Sometimes, this results in very interesting leathers. For example, snakeskin leather shows off the unique patterns of scales that cover a snake's body. These kinds of leather are often used to create flashy clothing. If you visit a store that specializes in cowboy boots, you'll probably catch a glimpse of just about every type of leather imaginable.

Many leatherworkers make goods and sell them
online or at craft fairs.

Other leatherworkers rely on interesting designs to make their creations stand out. Try looking at two leather belts. They might be the same general color and shape. But if you look carefully, you might notice that the edges of the leather are finished differently. Or the tip of the belt might be shaped differently at the end. Such details might not affect how useful or durable the object is. But even the smallest details can make something stand out.

Many artisans continue to practice traditional leatherworking methods.

Even with so many leather goods being manufactured by machines, a demand will always exist for skilled artisans who can create truly amazing things from leather. No machine can reproduce the detail and quality of handmade leather goods.

Inspiration Everywhere

You never know what might give you an idea for a new project. Maybe you are watching a movie when you see a character wearing something interesting that you'd like to try making. Or maybe you wish you had a carrying case for your sunglasses or something else you use all the time. Maybe an interesting shape simply pops into your head out of nowhere. Before you lose these ideas, sketch them in a notebook. Even if an idea seems silly or you're unsure it will work, go ahead and put it in your notes. Later, you can flip through the pages when you are trying to figure out what you want to make next.

Craft Activity

Design Your Own Leather Creation

You don't need a bunch of tools or expensive leather to start designing your own projects. The first steps of any leatherworking project are more about planning and designing, so put your creativity to work!

SUPPLIES

- Paper and pencil
- Ruler
- Scissors
- Tape

STEPS

1. Sketch out an idea for a small leather object. It could be a wallet, a phone case, or anything else you can think of.

2. Look carefully at your drawing. How would it be assembled? How many pieces of leather would you need? What shapes and sizes would they be?

3. Draw a pattern for the leather pieces on a fresh sheet of paper. Cut them out and use tape to assemble them.

4. Did your pieces fit together the way you planned? If not, make adjustments and try again. Once you get it right, you'll have a pattern for a future leather project.

Find Out More

BOOKS

Eastman, Linda Sue. *Leathercraft.* East Petersburg, PA: Fox Chapel Publishing, 2008.

Felix, Rebecca. *Cool Leatherworking Projects: Fun & Creative Workshop Activities.* Minneapolis, MN: ABDO Publishing, 2017.

WEBSITES

U.S. Bureau of Labor Statistics Occupational Outlook Handbook—Craft and Fine Artists
www.bls.gov/ooh/arts-and-design/craft-and-fine-artists.htm
Check out official data about employment rates, average salaries, and more for professional artisans.

YouTube—Corter Leather
www.youtube.com/c/CorterLeather/videos
Watch dozens of videos of artisans making truly unique leather objects.

GLOSSARY

apprenticeship (uh-PREN-tiss-ship) an arrangement where an inexperienced worker trains with someone more experienced

artisan (AR-tuh-zuhn) someone who is skilled at working with their hands on a specific craft

awl (AWL) a pointed tool used for poking holes in leather or other materials

bacteria (bak-TIHR-ee-uh) microscopic, single-celled life that exist almost everywhere

burnish (BUHR-nish) to rub something until it begins to darken and shine

chisel (CHIZ-uhl) a tool with a long, flat blade that can be used to cut, scrape, or chip at things

cobbler (KAH-bluhr) someone who makes or repairs shoes by hand

efficient (uh-FISH-uhnt) able to produce work with minimal waste of time or material

exotic (eg-ZAH-tik) rare or uncommon

hide (HYDE) the skin of a large animal

organic (or-GAN-ik) related to a living thing

upholstering (uhp-HOL-stuhr-ing) covering furniture with fabric, leather, or other materials

versatile (VUR-suh-tuhl) useful in many ways

INDEX

apprenticeships, 22–23
awl, 18

belts, 17
burnishing, 19

chisel, 18
clicking, 16–17
clothing, leather, 25, 26
cobblers, 23
conditioning, 19
craft activity, 30
creativity, 20
cutting, 14, 16, 17

detail, attention to, 13

gluing, 18

hides, 8, 14–15

inspiration, 29

knives, 19

leather/leatherworking
    adding details to, 19
    beginning a project, 12–13

as a career, 20–25
caring for, 16
choosing which leather
    to use, 14–15
cleaning, 16, 19
colors, 8, 24
controversies about, 11
craft activity, 30
cutting, 14, 16, 17
design details, 27
designing a pattern, 13–14
exotic, 26
history of, 4
introduction, 4–11
joining pieces of, 18
as luxury item, 11
manufacturing, 10
polishing, 16, 19
popularity of, 4–6
preventing waste, 15–16
repairing, 19
setting a price for items, 25
sewing, 9, 18
tanning, 7–8, 10, 14, 24
tools, 10, 17–19
traditional methods, 28
types of projects, 26–29
what it's used for, 6, 7, 10–11

leatherworker
    apprenticeships, 22–23
    education, 22
    inspiration, 29
    lifestyle, 12–19
    necessary skills and assets,
        20–21
    practicing basic skills, 22
    specialized skills, 23
    where jobs are, 25

money management, 25

patterns, 13–14
polishing, 16, 19
punch, 17

repairs, 19
rotary hole punch, 17

saddle stitching, 18
samples, 14
sewing machines, 9, 18
snakeskin, 26
stitching, saddle, 18

tanning, 7–8, 10, 14, 24
tools, 10, 17–19

upholstering, 23